high up in the mountains . . .

on an island . . .

in Japan.

To Mary Lentz, a California reader of
other books in this series, who first told
me about Kamikatsu—thank you!
And to Shoko Nagashima,
who was first to read my story.

Farrar Straus Giroux Books for Young Readers
An imprint of Macmillan Publishing Group, LLC
120 Broadway, New York, NY 10271 • mackids.com

Our books may be purchased in bulk for promotional, educational, or business
use. Please contact your local bookseller or the Macmillan Corporate and
Premium Sales Department at (800) 221-7945 ext. 5442 or by email at
MacmillanSpecialMarkets@macmillan.com.

Library of Congress Control Number: 2022910013

First edition, 2023
Book design by Mike Burroughs
Color separations by Altaimage Corp
Printed in China by RR Donnelley Asia Printing Solutions Ltd.,
Dongguan City, Guangdong Province

ISBN 978-0-374-38840-9
1 3 5 7 9 10 8 6 4 2

Flower!

Bird!

Wind!

Moon!

allan drummond

zero waste

How One Community Is Leading a World Recycling Revolution

Farrar Straus Giroux
New York

Kamikatsu, Japan, is an old-fashioned kind of place.
Not much happens here, or so it seems.

Our grandma has lived in Kamikatsu all her life.
In fact, there are a lot of older people here.

Bye!

Hello, you young ones!

When we come to stay at her house, she loves to teach
us old-fashioned Japanese words and proverbs.

"Flower, bird, wind, moon," she says. "Kachou fuugetsu!"

Huh...

Uh?

As usual, at first she leaves us to
work out what she means.

Kachou fuugetsu!

What's that?

"Kachou fuugetsu? To me, it means, 'Experience the
beauty of nature. Learn about yourself!'" she explains.

Okay. Good night, Grandma!

The next day is recycling day for the people in Kamikatsu, and in the morning Grandma is sorting out her trash. We are eager to help.

"Okay!" she says. "Here are my nine bins for nine different kinds of waste paper! Let's go!"

Cardboard,

Snap!

newspaper,

"Oh, and here are five more bins for metal waste!" she says.

Aluminum cans, steel cans, spray cans,

caps, and scrap metal.

"Then my six bins for glass recycling!"

Clear glass, green glass, brown glass, mirror glass, light bulbs, pottery.

"And other bins for old batteries, for rubber, and for fabric."

Suddenly Grandma grabs hold of us and gives us a huge hug.
"Well done! You've got it! Reduce, reuse, and recycle!"
Then she adds another proverb.

A truck comes to collect the trash from older citizens like Grandma. We follow the truck as it goes to the recycling center. Recycling day is always exciting in Kamikatsu.

You see, here, everyone in the town tries to recycle everything. It may seem like not much happens in Kamikatsu, but this community is trying to do something very special.

It's called Zero Waste.

Zero Waste is Kamikatsu's big idea. And it's an idea that could change the world. The goal is to try to recycle everything. For more than twenty years now, Zero Waste has been the aim of everyone in town.

And recently the whole world has taken notice.

THE IDEA OF ZERO WASTE

Most of us know the word *recycle*. And most of us think we know what it means—taking care of our waste and sorting out things like plastic, glass, and metal to be collected so the material can go on to have a new life. It's a word that lots of people use. But we don't really question the idea of recycling. In fact, lots of us don't ask any questions about our waste.

If you look closely at the picture here, you'll see that the Kamikatsu Zero Waste Center is shaped like a giant question mark. There's a reason for that.

The idea behind the project is that we should always be asking really big questions about the things we all use. We should be asking things like, *Where do the things we use come from? Why do we buy them? And where do they go when we are finished with them?* Today, in many parts of the world, we produce, buy, and use far too many things, and then we throw them away. This behavior is wasteful. It uses up energy and materials. It's what is called unsustainable, meaning it can't go on. We could end up running out of the materials our things are made of. Aiming for Zero Waste means we're aiming for sustainability.

Grandma tells us that back when she was a young mom, she threw things away without thinking.

"Like everyone here, I wanted our family's waste to just disappear. To be invisible."

Clang!

Gone!

Gone!

Goodbye!

People in Kamikatsu would drag their trash to a great big hole in the ground.

Job done!

Good riddance!

Much of what came up the hill to Kamikatsu eventually ended up in the big hole—thousands of plastic bags, paper cartons, plastic bottles, clothes, old toys, food waste, garden rubbish, rubber, electronics, mattresses, furniture . . . literally anything.

As the hole filled up, people just made it bigger and bigger.

People also took their trash to the town's two incinerators, where it burned all day and all night, filling the mountain air with filthy smoke and horrible gases.

Some days it felt like their whole world was choking with waste.

The stink was awful.

Often the valleys filled with the smell of burning trash. The river and the streams became polluted.

Like a lot of small, remote towns in Japan, Kamikatsu was not considered big enough to have a waste-collection service.

Many residents could not bring their trash to the pit or the incinerators, so they burned their garbage out in the open, right beside their houses.

Cough! Sputter!

That got rid of it!

Gasp!

Grandma worried that someday she might not see a flower . . .

or hear a bird . . .

and that the wind

would carry poisonous black clouds across the moon.

"So much for kachou fuugetsu," said Grandma.

Moon!

"Experience the beauty of nature? Learn about yourself? That's not happening here. Something has to be done."

And then scientists came and discovered a problem bigger than just smoke and smell. They found poisonous dioxins in the air, the soil, and the water—all because of the burning and dumping of the town's waste.

So the town decided to close the incinerators and trash pit. There was to be no more burning or dumping of waste in Kamikatsu. Trash would have to be taken to sites farther away for disposal—too far for many residents.

And rubbish started to pile up.

WASTE CAN CAUSE BIG PROBLEMS

Many of us are lucky enough to live in places where our waste is picked up and taken away. Once our rubbish is dropped down a chute in an apartment building or put in a bag or can and taken to the curb for sanitation workers to haul off, we don't have to think about it anymore. But for most of the population of the world—for millions and millions of people—this is not the case. Most people on the planet, particularly in poor and remote places, lack trash-collection services and must burn their waste out in the open or dump their waste in landfills themselves. They don't have a choice.

Burning waste causes air pollution— smoke and fumes that have harmful effects on humans, animals, and plants. Burning also releases carbon dioxide, the greenhouse gas that is filling our atmosphere and warming our climate. When waste burns, it can make all kinds of poisonous gases as well. Dioxins are one poison commonly produced when waste is not handled properly. Dioxins build up in our bodies and in animals' bodies, causing serious health problems.

Dumping waste on or in the ground can also cause massive problems. Rainwater and water in the ground can wash out dangerous chemicals that get into rivers and the water supply. And a lot of the waste just stays where it is, causing huge buildups of material and the stinky gases they release while decaying.

REDUCE, REUSE, RECYCLE

These three activities seem similar, but when we really think about each word, we get to the heart of the idea behind Zero Waste.

Reduce
First, if we really focus on reducing the things we consume—from using less paper to not taking more food than we can eat—then we automatically reduce our waste. This is a big step toward sustainability, which basically means not using up everything.

Reuse
We all love having something "new." But the word *new* can mean something that is new to us or something that has been given a new use. It's just like when we reuse or hand down old clothes and furniture. Or when we upcycle trash into treasure by turning things like an old plastic bottle into a toy storage bin, egg cartons into craft supplies, or scraps of wood into a bookshelf. Thinking about how we can reuse something is also at the heart of Zero Waste.

Recycle
For waste, this means knowing what can be done with the things we use once we are finished with them. It's easy to imagine used glass and metal being melted down to make new glass and metal objects. But imagine if the bottles and tins and cartons that we use were all made with recycling in mind right from the start. This does happen a lot—but so much more can be done. Again, if we really focus on the meaning of recycling, we get closer to Zero Waste.

"I remember it very well," Grandma says. "The small town of Kamikatsu now had a big waste problem."

People had to start looking seriously at reducing, reusing, and recycling the waste. Either that, or the town would die.

Of course, back then everyone knew about recycling, but not many people actually did it. A lot of talking had to happen.

All kinds of people spoke up—including Grandma, who started with her proverbs.

For three years people worked hard at recycling. It was tough going.

A big new recycling center was built. But to use it, people had to first sort their waste.

Not everyone was happy.

People had to identify nearly fifty different types of waste.

"It's too much!" some said. "We'll need so many different bins!"
Once again, it seemed impossible.

But what came next was extraordinary.
In 2003 the town made a Zero Waste Declaration.
It promised that by 2020 Kamikatsu would become the world's first Zero Waste Town. Its residents would reduce waste, reuse every last bit of garbage, and recycle.

It was a very big idea for a small town. And a very big promise.
Was a Zero Waste Town even possible?

Well, at this time, all over the world, the problem of waste had started to become big news.

Everywhere, people were realizing that they had the same waste problem as the small town of Kamikatsu.

The open burning of waste . . .

dioxins in the air, water, and soil . . .

plastic in the ocean . . .

People all over the planet were realizing that the problem of waste would not go away and that we all have a part to play in solving the problem.

And just then Kamikatsu's Zero Waste efforts started making the news . . .

That's a great idea!

zero waste

Suddenly the whole world was interested in the small town of Kamikatsu. They watched as the community took on the challenge of Zero Waste.

It's a lot of work!

Let's go!

The news attracted visitors from many countries.

Kamikatsu

Some young people have stayed and made the town their home. Grandma likes having them as neighbors.

Hello!

Kachou fuugetsu!

The beauty of nature.

Learn about yourself!

The Kamikatsu Zero Waste Academy was started. It's where people can learn about the best steps to take toward achieving Zero Waste in their towns. In 2020 a young woman named Akira Sakano, the new director of the waste academy, was invited to the World Economic Forum to tell the world about the town's Zero Waste project.

Kamikatsu and its Zero Waste project had arrived on the world stage.

Visitors here always ask, "Has Kamikatsu achieved its dream of becoming a Zero Waste Town?"
And the people dropping off their waste after sorting it all out know the answer.

Well, the community manages to recycle more than 80 percent of its waste.

We know that's not everything. But if the whole world did this . . .

It would make a huge difference!

Today Kamikatsu is rightly proud of its achievements. It's still a small, old-fashioned, quiet place in the mountains.

But something big has happened here. A Zero Waste plan started with this community, and it has spread around the world.

At the Zero Waste Academy, there's a classroom where children come from far and wide to learn about the Zero Waste project.

Wow!

And there's a shop selling reusable items large and small. It's called Kurukuru, which in Japanese means going around and around. It can also mean working hard.

KURUKURU

Waste not, want not!

Mottainai!

So the words *reduce*, *reuse*, and *recycle* are at the heart of the Zero Waste idea.

Next door, there's even a hotel where people can stay.
The building is made entirely of recycled materials.

In Kamikatsu guests are welcomed from all over the world and can experience the beauty of nature. Streams and a river flow nearby. The air is fresh, and you can clearly see the mountains. On an evening walk you might feel a breeze, hear birdsong, look at flowers, and see the moon rising through the pine trees.

LEFT PAGE: [TOP] A Kamikatsu resident (at right) laughs as she chats with a staff member at the recycling center while sorting her household waste (Carl Court/Getty Images). [BOTTOM] A worker sorts newspapers and magazines (Kazuhiro Nogi/AFPB via Getty Images). RIGHT PAGE: [TOP] Bins for eight of the nearly fifty categories of waste into which residents and workers sort their trash (Carl Court/Getty Images). [BOTTOM] The Kamikatsu waste recycling facility is shaped like a question mark, reflecting the questions we should all be asking about how best to dispose of our trash (Carl Court/Getty Images).

AUTHOR'S NOTE

Can we live in society without producing any waste? It's a great question to ask ourselves. And it's a great discussion to have with friends and classmates. Try it!

We see from Kamikatsu's story that it is very hard indeed to get to Zero Waste. On its journey the community has raised lots of different questions and found lots of different answers. There is no doubt that taking steps toward Zero Waste offers many benefits. Try listing them!

One important message from Kamikatsu is, "Think before you trash!" If we each do this, we begin to play our own personal part in dealing with our waste in the best way possible. But what about this idea: "Think before you buy!"? This is something that Akira Sakano, first director of the Zero Waste Academy, likes to say. If we start thinking before we buy something, then we can have an effect on the people and companies that make the things we buy. Things can be made or wrapped differently to reduce waste. There's a lot to talk about when it comes to understanding how ordinary decisions we all make every day can have an immediate and powerful impact on eliminating waste from our lives.

Once you start exploring the idea of Zero Waste, you will find lots of interesting stories and resources, including many videos and news stories online. Below I've listed a few resources that may be intriguing. Chiritsumo!

FOR FURTHER READING

These are some of the resources I found very useful as the COVID-19 pandemic prevented me from traveling to Japan.

Gray, Alex. "The Inspiring Thing That Happened When a Japanese Village Went Almost Waste-Free." World Economic Forum. January 21, 2019. weforum.org/agenda/2019/01/the-inspiring-thing-that-happened-when-a-japanese-village-went-almost-waste-free/.

Lee, Michelle Ye Hee and Julia Mio Inuma. "Postcards from Kamikatsu, Japan's 'Zero-Waste' Town." *The Washington Post.* April 27, 2022. washingtonpost.com/climate-solutions/interactive/2022/japan-zero-carbon-village-climate/.

Parras, Patricia. "Small Town, Big Steps: The Story of Kamikatsu, Japan." Global Alliance for Incinerator Alternatives. 2019. zerowasteworld.org/wp-content/uploads/Japan.pdf.

Experience the beauty of nature.

Learn about yourself.